Ancient Civilizations For Kids

A History Series

Children Explore History Book Edition

SPEEDY
PUBLISHING

FUN FACTS

about the
EGYPTIAN, GREEK
and ROMAN
ANCIENT
CIVILIZATION

Most Ancient Egyptian pyramids were built as tombs for pharaohs and their families.

Egyptians believed that by preserving a dead person's body their soul would live on in the after-life forever.

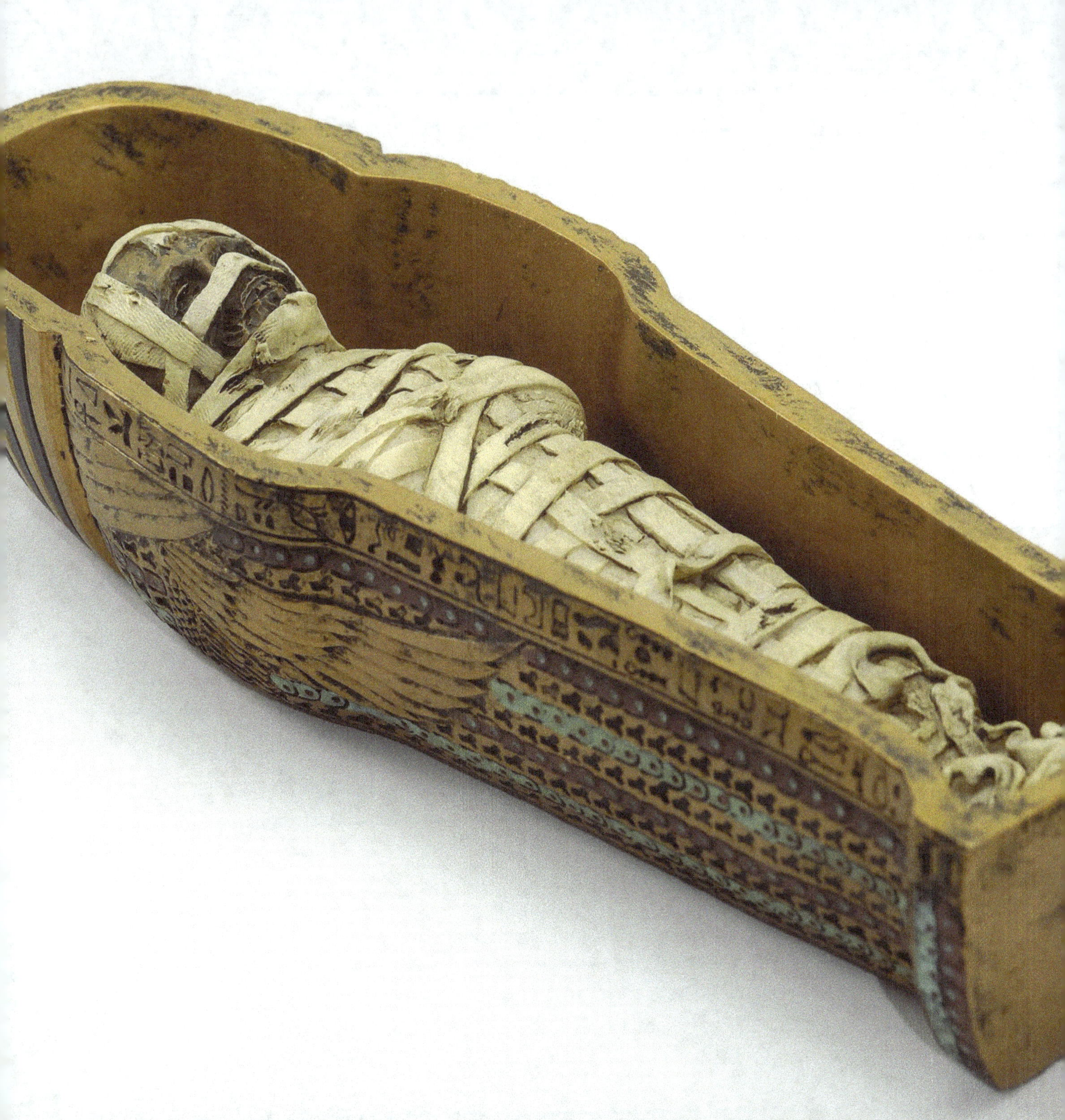

The **Egyptian** alphabet contained more than 700 hieroglyphs!

The **Egyptians** believed makeup had magical healing powers!

Cats were considered to be a sacred animal by the Ancient Egyptians.

The Pyramid of
Khufu at Giza
is the largest
Egyptian pyramid.

The **Greeks** had some strange superstitions about food some wouldn't eat beans as they thought they contained the souls of the dead!

Events at the **Greek's** Olympics included wrestling, boxing, long jump, javelin, discus and chariot racing.

The **Greeks** put statues of their gods inside temples, the most famous of which is the Parthenon.

Ancient **Greeks** loved watching plays, and most cities had a theatre.

The Ancient Greeks held many festivals in honour of their gods. To celebrate the god Zeus, for example, the first Greek Olympics.

Rome was founded in 753BC by its first king, Romulus.

The **Roman** Empire included the whole of Italy, all the lands around the Mediterranean and much of Europe.

The **Romans** built such a huge empire and conquered new lands because of their strong army.

The **Romans** didn't spend all their time fighting – they were amazing architects and engineers too as they buildt road and walls.

To bring water to their cities, the clever Romans built aqueducts.

The **Romans** believed in gods and goddesses who ruled over different areas of life.

The **Romans** liked to enjoy their food, often lying down on a couch while eating with their hands.

MVLSVM

Visit
BABY PROFESSOR
EDUCATION KIDS
www.BabyProfessorBooks.com
to download Free Baby Professor eBooks
and view our catalog of new and exciting
Children's Books

www.ingramcontent.com/pod-product-compliance
Lightning Source LLC
Chambersburg PA
CBHW081149180726
48003CB00026B/2991